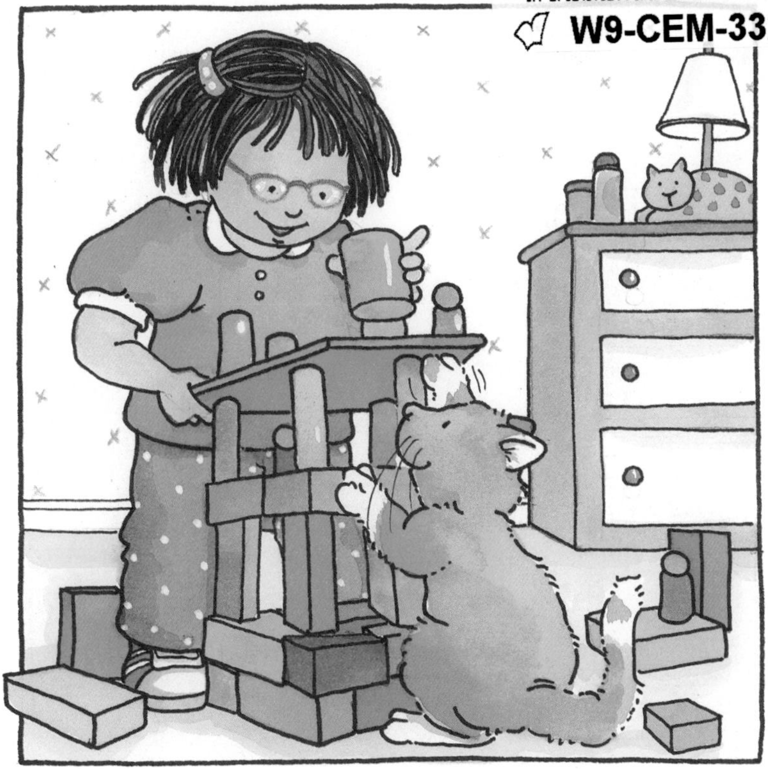

I play with blocks.

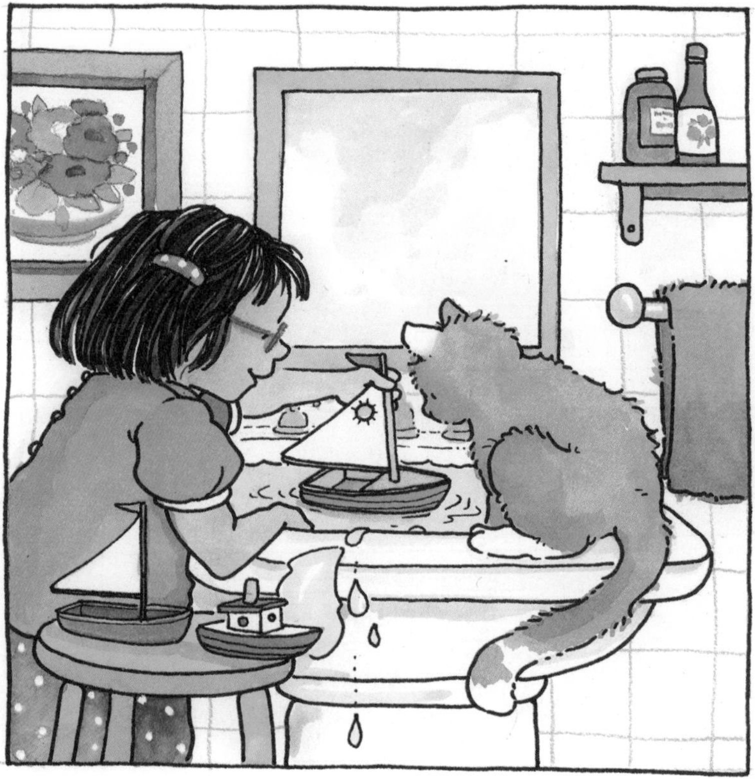

I play with boats.

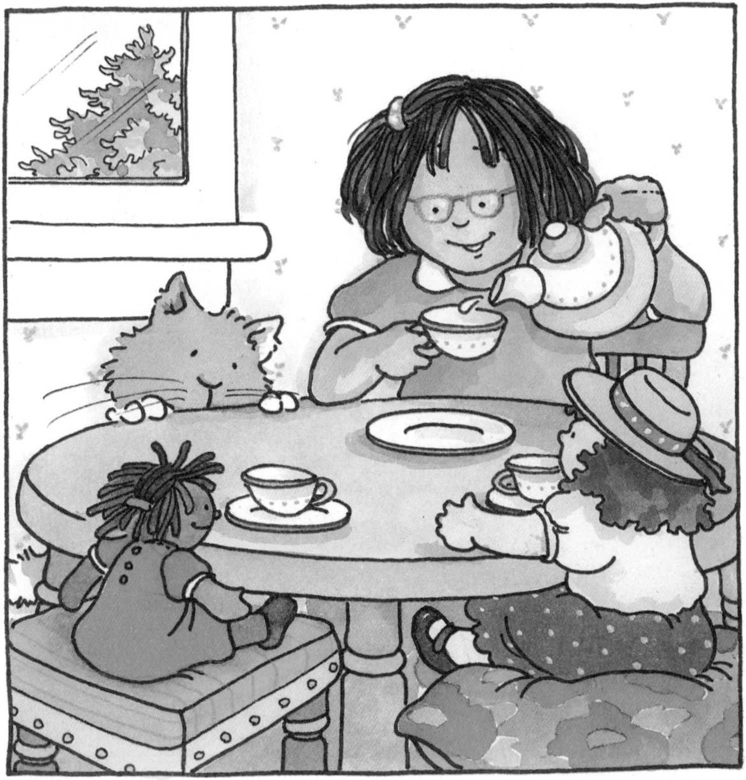

I play with dolls.

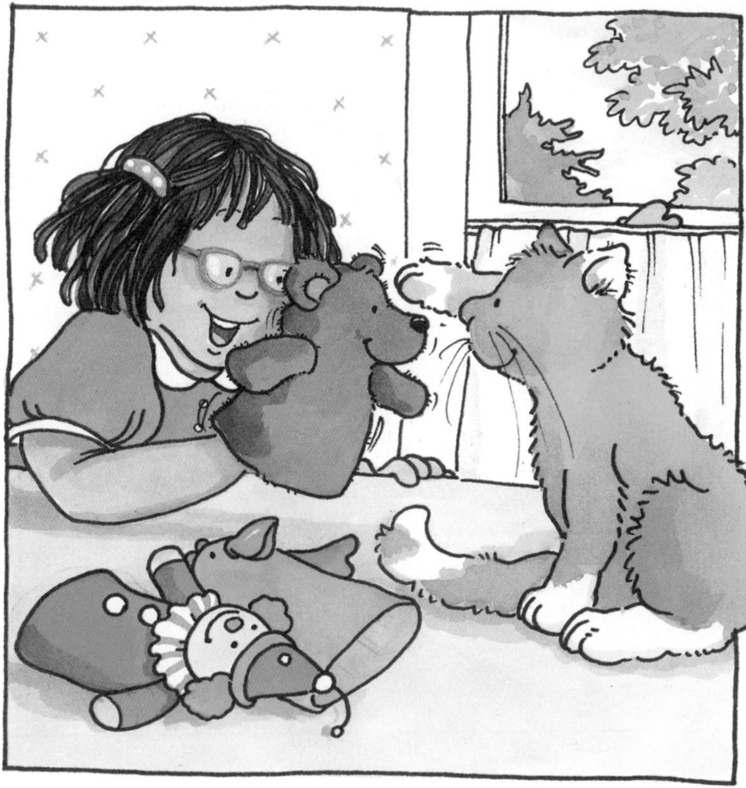

I play with puppets.

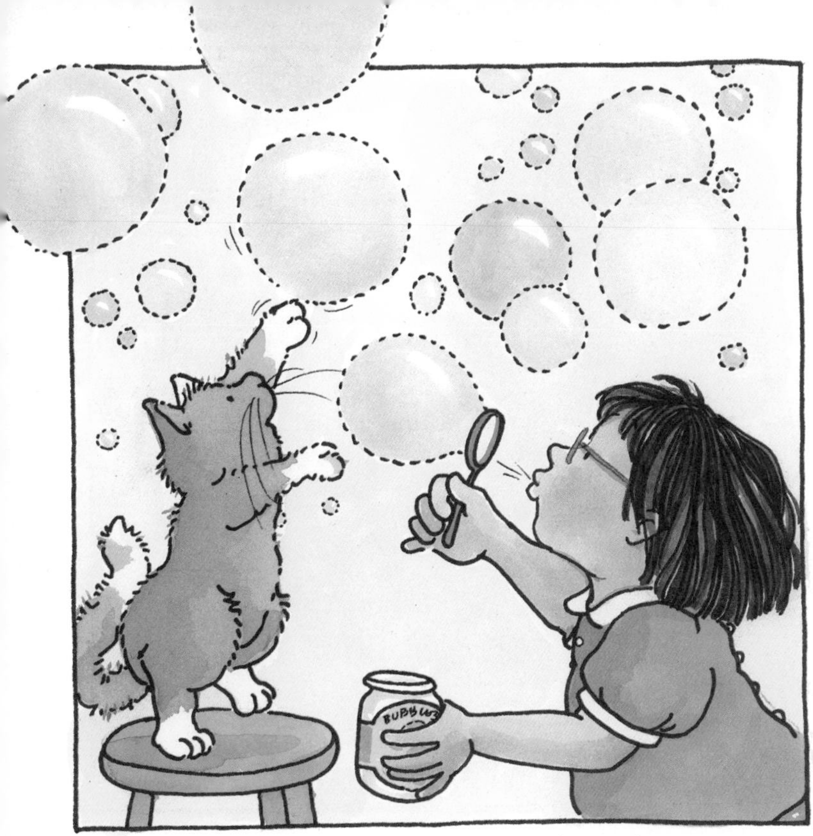

I play with bubbles.

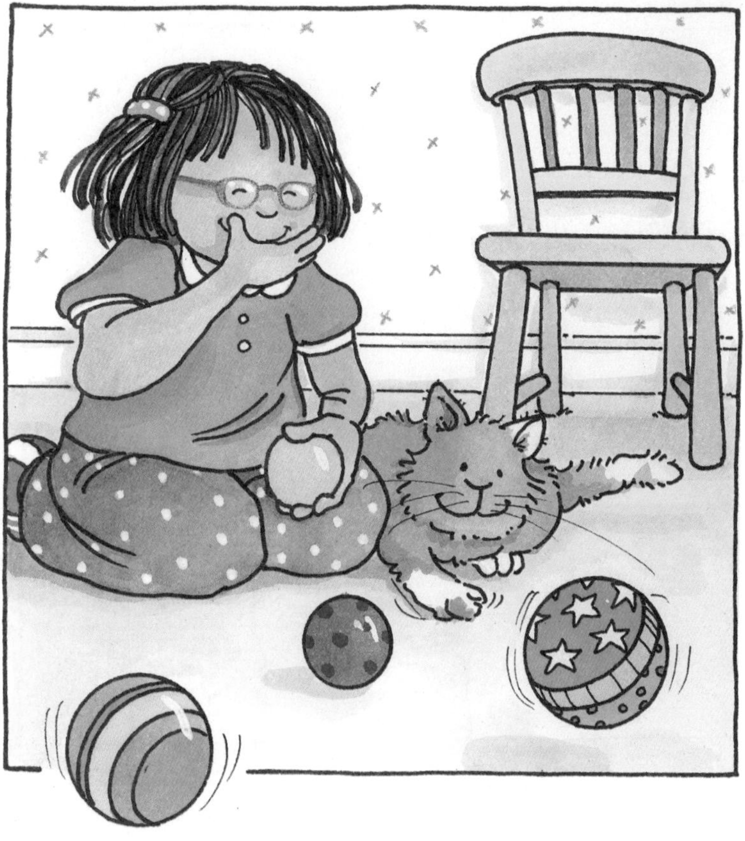

I play with balls.

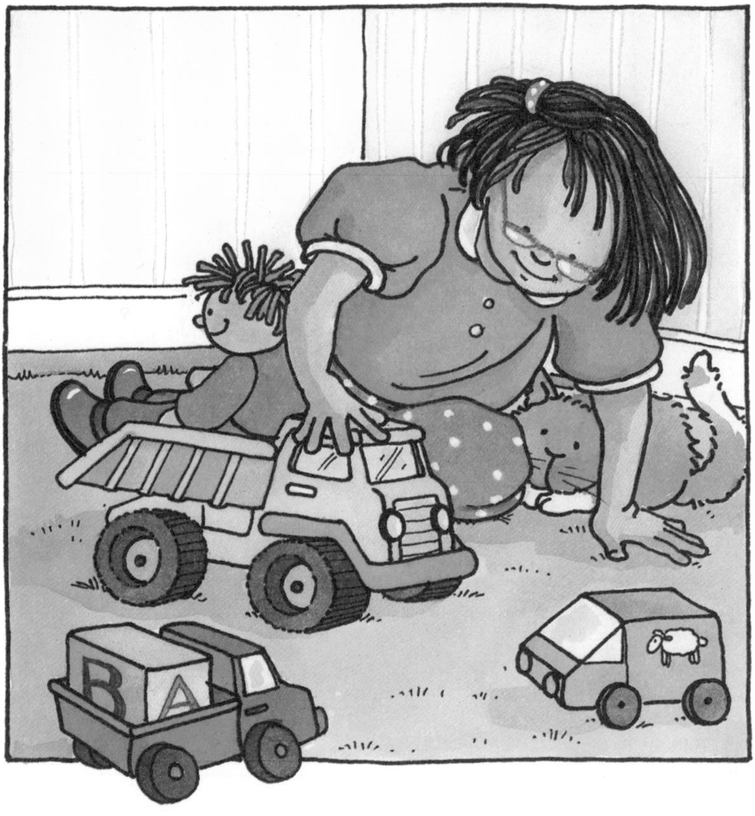


I play with trucks.

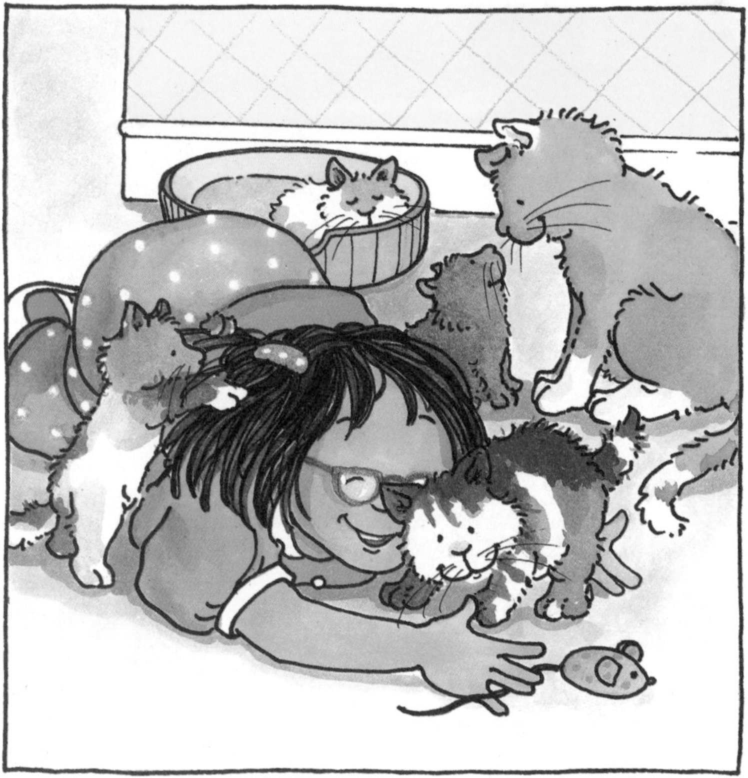

I play with kittens!